WARTIME NEWCASTLE-und LYME

by

DAVE ADAMS

Scrap Iron.   This military tank, a memento of the First World War, was removed shortly before the Second World War for scrap iron. It was a popular playground for local children. The Crimean War cannon which stood nearby was also sought by the Ministry of Supply in April 1941, but in view of the historical nature of the weapon the council refused.

Published by Hendon Publishing Co. Ltd., Hendon Mill, Nelson, Lancashire
Text © Dave Adams, 1988
Printed by Fretwell & Cox Ltd., Goulbourne Street, Keighley, West Yorkshire BD21 1PZ

INTRODUCTION

In 1986, whilst contemplating a subject for an exhibition of local history photographs at Newcastle Library, I decided to display some of the wartime photographs that were in the library's collection. Within a few days of the opening of the exhibition, that collection was greatly augmented. Memories and memorabilia of the Second World War play a great part in the lives of those who lived through it. Local people brought photographs by the dozen, together with ration books, posters, ARP instructions etc. into the library in order for us to display.

So successful was the exhibition that when I was asked by the publisher of this book to write an illustrated history of wartime Newcastle I had no hesitation in accepting. As I was born in 1946 my initial task was to talk to old Newcastillians who had lived here during the 1930s and 1940s. The first person I interviewed, when told the subject of the book, said that the average Newcastle resident 'didn't know that the war was on'. My subsequent researches and the photographic evidence which follows hopefully prove him wrong. The fact that Newcastle escaped the blitz does not mean that it escaped loss of loved ones, rationing, black-outs, ARP, fire watching, evacuees, U.S. soldiers, conscription and other wartime experiences.

D. W. Adams

March 1988

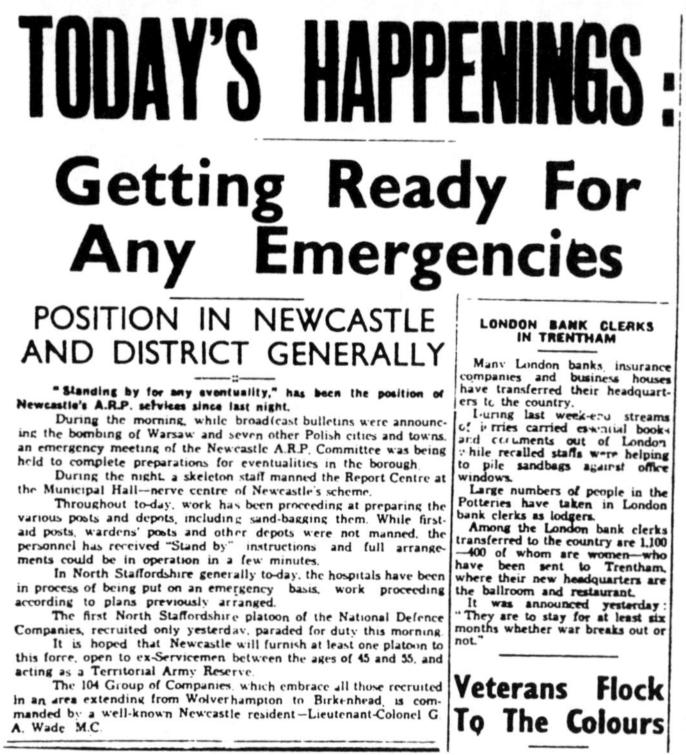

TODAY'S HAPPENINGS :

Getting Ready For Any Emergencies

POSITION IN NEWCASTLE AND DISTRICT GENERALLY

"**Standing by for any eventuality**," has been the position of Newcastle's A.R.P. services since last night.

During the morning, while broadcast bulletins were announcing the bombing of Warsaw and seven other Polish cities and towns, an emergency meeting of the Newcastle A.R.P. Committee was being held to complete preparations for eventualities in the borough.

During the night, a skeleton staff manned the Report Centre at the Municipal Hall—nerve centre of Newcastle's scheme.

Throughout to-day, work has been proceeding at preparing the various posts and depots, including sand-bagging them. While first-aid posts, wardens' posts and other depots were not manned, the personnel has received "Stand by" instructions and full arrangements could be in operation in a few minutes.

In North Staffordshire generally to-day, the hospitals have been in process of being put on an emergency basis, work proceeding according to plans previously arranged.

The first North Staffordshire platoon of the National Defence Companies, recruited only yesterday, paraded for duty this morning.

It is hoped that Newcastle will furnish at least one platoon to this force, open to ex-Servicemen between the ages of 45 and 55, and acting as a Territorial Army Reserve.

The 104 Group of Companies, which embrace all those recruited in an area extending from Wolverhampton to Birkenhead, is commanded by a well-known Newcastle resident—Lieutenant-Colonel G. A. Wade M.C.

LONDON BANK CLERKS IN TRENTHAM

Many London banks, insurance companies and business houses have transferred their headquarters to the country.

During last week-end streams of lorries carried essential books and documents out of London while recalled staffs were helping to pile sandbags against office windows.

Large numbers of people in the Potteries have taken in London bank clerks as lodgers.

Among the London bank clerks transferred to the country are 1,100—400 of whom are women—who have been sent to Trentham, where their new headquarters are the ballroom and restaurant.

It was announced yesterday : "They are to stay for at least six months whether war breaks out or not."

Veterans Flock To The Colours

Getting Ready. Headline news from the *Newcastle Times* of 1st September 1939.

First Aid. Pictured here are the medical staff from Silverdale First Aid Post which was situated in the council school building.

Rubbish. Even the most mundane of household chores was affected by the war (September 1939).

Information. The wartime Information Centre which occupied part of Hayden's shop on the corner of High Street and Friars Street.

Allotments Committee.

Present :—Councillor Leech (in the Chair) ; Alderman Heywood, Mayor ; Alderman Bentley ; Councillors Davies, Mrs. Deakin, Mrs. Gater, Hamner, and Tinsdill ; Messrs. Gilmore, Ikins, Wilkes and Cook.

Apology.

1.   An apology for absence was received from Alderman Saunders.

Cultivation of Allotments—War Time.

2.   The Chairman referred to a recent interview which the Mayor had had with Lord Harrowby on this matter. The Mayor stated that Lord Harrowby as President of the County Allotment Holders' Association was most anxious that an immediate appeal should be made to the public with a view to stimulating interest and also for increasing the number of allotments for food production during the period of the present War. He had therefore asked the Chairman to call a Special Meeting for the purpose of discussing the matter with a view to taking measures to this end. The Committee subsequently fully discussed the matter.

> (a) That a Special Appeal be made in the names of Lord Harrowby and the Mayor for the public support and interest on the lines suggested by the Committee.

Resolved :—

> (b) That the following concessions be granted during the period of the War :—
>
> 1. To the tenants of existing Corporation allotments—a concession of half rent during the period of the War.
>
> 2. To grant the tenancy of approximately 50 existing vacant allotments in the Borough free for the first 12 months and thereafter at half the rent usually charged for same during the period of the war.
>
> 3. To immediately acquire additional land for cultivation in any part of the Borough including the Westlands Estate if the applications received warrant the same.
>
> 4. That no tenant at present occupying an allotment be allowed to transfer to another allotment.

Wartime Scenes (1).   Ashley's Square, off Brook Lane, 1940.

Air Raid Precautions.   On the right of this High Street photograph, probably taken just after the war, can be seen an air raid shelter sign (by the cinema).

Fire Brigade (1).   A wartime procession by Newcastle firemen entering Ironmarket from Nelson Place.

Fire Brigade (2).   Newcastle firemen ready for action outside the fire station in King Street.

Auxiliary Fire Brigade. Members of Chesterton Auxiliary Fire Brigade. The Newcastle Auxiliary Fire Station was situated in Goose Street.

Wartime Scenes (2).   Penkhull Street, looking towards Stubbs Gate. The sign on the wall by the two cars reads 'Freedom is in peril, defend it with all your might.' (1940)

Fund Raising (1). The Spitfire designed by local man, R.J. Mitchell, inspired local people to raise money towards the purchase of the aircraft. This shows the winning design in the Sentinel poster competition.

"SPITFIRE CORNER"

"On to the second thousand," is on the lips of every Spitfire enthusiast in the borough, and the Deputy Mayor (Councillor George A. Heywood), in his capacity as chairman of Newcastle's Spitfire Fund, has set an admirable lead with the slogan "He gives twice who gives quickly."

Only eight days to reach the £1,000 mark is good going, but efforts are not to be slackened, for speed is on obvious necessity.

By the courtesy of the Newcastle Corporation, the fund has been granted the use of a shop on the Island Site, to be known as "Spitfire Corner," where contributions will be gladly received

The garden party held at Red Heath, Silverdale, realised £101 and a contribution of £13 has been received through Mr. L. G. Fetzer, Secretary of Newcastle Chamber of Trade, from the Globe Cafe, Ltd., High-street.

To-morrow and Monday the "Mile of Shillings" effort will take place.

At the committee's request, Wolstanton Traders' Association are organising local efforts on behalf of the fund, to embrace Wolstanton, May Bank and Porthill districts.

Fund Raising (2). News of progress for Newcastle's Spitfire fund, 6th September 1940.

Enemy Action (1). Newcastle suffered isolated bombing incidents. Mainly they were from off-course raiders or attempts on the Shelton Bar complex. This photo shows damage to the May Bank area on the 2nd June 1941.

Enemy Action (2).   On the afternoon of 14th December 1940 a lone German aircraft dropped a stick of bombs on the village of Chesterton. There was extensive damage to property and numerous casualties.

Enemy Action (3). The Chesterton Salvation Army worked through the night and the following day, providing food and hot drinks for the rescue workers.

Is Your Journey Really Necessary? A PMT bus in Newcastle. The reduced destination board was a typical feature of wartime buses.

Playing Fields.

All senior schools should have a playing-field within reach of them, where they can take the Organised Games lesson more satisfactorily. The Westlands possess two very good grass pitches of their own, and the Orme playing field for the Newcastle schools is being enlarged and should be a fine ground when the work is complete. Knutton have their own ground too, and all these three fields can be truly appreciated in fine weather. Chesterton and Silverdale have fields, but not in such satisfactory conditions ; but there is no suitable pitch for the Wolstanton schools. It seems a pity, when the other areas are provided for, that a site cannot be rescued before building processes swallow them up, for the Watlands Senior School, Wolstanton C.E. and Ellison Street Schools to appropriate for their ground. The major games of Football, Hockey, Field Hand-ball or Rounders cannot be successfully taught unless there is a decent field suitably near to the school, and I should like all Senior schools to have equal opportunity of playing one or other of these games, and the Junior schools of leading up to them.

Incidentally the air-raid shelters will be a boon on the playing fields, because they may also be used as pavilions of a temporary kind, and hitherto, the grounds lacked these. If schools are to be encouraged to use the playing fields, there needs to be some shelter accommodation for the children and somewhere to store the equipment.

Equipment.

In war-time the cost of equipment is greatly increased, and naturally economy has to be studied so the schools cannot be provided with as much as one would desire, but on the whole what they have is in fairly good condition.

The personal equipment of the children is a more difficult problem, because a great many boys and girls cannot afford rubber shoes of their own for their physical training lesson, and unsuitable footgear greatly diminishes the value of the work. The provision of shoes is the first essential equipment necessary for all children. Some years ago the Committee made a liberal grant of about 3,000 pairs of shoes, which proved a great blessing for some of the poorer children in the schools, but most of this supply is worn out now, and more shoes are needed. It is hoped that some means of providing them will be adopted.

St. Patrick's Senior School are making a special dress for their girls to wear for physical training. This is an excellent plan, and the more the girls and boys can be encouraged to strip or to wear a special uniform, the better are the results likely to be. Teachers are trying to educate the children to wear suitable clothes and garments, and in this respect they can give much valuable hygienic advice which is sorely needed.

Recreational and Post-School Classes.

This winter no Keep-Fit Classes or Teachers' classes have been held, and the evening institutes have been closed due to the "blacking-out" problems. Many of the teachers and members too were engaged in A.R.P. and other war-time duties. But physical fitness should be encouraged, rather than the reverse, in war time and next winter it is hoped that the work will be resumed. Previously, there had been several flourishing classes in the district. Newcastle would benefit by possessing some Central Hall or Gymnasium, where the youth of the town could go for enjoyment and training. In Mr. Lindsay's lecture "The Service of Youth", he urged us to try and cater more for the post-school

Out Of Adversity. Extract from the school medical officer's report for 1939. He found air raid shelters to be a boon when used as pavilions. Note his encouragement for boys and girls to strip.

R.O.F. Radway Green. Although not situated in Newcastle, many local women travelled to work in the armaments factories at Radway Green and Swynnerton. The ladies pictured here are having a well-earned celebration.

War Workers. The NAAFI supply depot at the North Staffs Brickyard, Chesterton, 1942.

Enderley Mills. Founded in the nineteenth century, upon the bankruptcy of its founder it was taken over by John Hammond and Co. Wars in Sudan and South Africa led to increased production of uniforms. The firm supplied millions of uniforms during both world wars, including those for the civil defence. This photograph shows a group of machinists during the Second World War. They are, left to right:
back row: Josey Evans, Violet Haynes, Mrs Betty Brown (GI bride), Hettie Hassall, Clarice Daniels, Ethel Ward. Gertie Wright
second row: Nancy Deakin, May Ratcliffe, Millie Smith, Freda Price, Dora Nicholls
front row: Clarice Booth, Joyce Eardley, Margaret Hughes, Mrs Joan Provan (GI bride), Hilda Myott, Ivy Bailey

B.S.A., Rolls Royce, Rist's. Second World War technology led to the setting up of mechanised production lines, which were devoted to the mass manufacture of one or two components only. Numerous similar production lines would feed large scale sub assembly and final assembly plants.

The B.S.A. Gun Company was bombed out of Birmingham in 1940 before their Newcastle factory was ready. An agency factory making parts for aircraft cannons for them had been approved in 1939, but was not brought into operation until April 1941. Rolls Royce, already in the area at Fenton and Stoke, took over the B.S.A. factory in 1944 to increase their production capacity. When Rolls Royce vacated the plant in February 1946 it was taken over by Rist's, who remain there today.

British Thompson Houston.   Rearmament began in 1934. Some areas of the country were more vulnerable to the possibility of air raids than others. North Staffordshire was the nearest large population cluster in a safe area close to the vulnerable West Midland conurbation. Two agency factories came to Newcastle; the second largest was for the British Thompson Houston Company of Rugby to augment their existing shell-producing capacity. At its peak the factory employed 340 males and 1360 females. After the war British Thompson Houston kept on its lease and decided to stay in Newcastle.

Wartime Scenes (3). The Ironmarket and Municipal Hall in 1943. Life as usual?

The Worshipful the Mayor of
    Newcastle-under-Lyme,
The Mayor's Parlour,
The Town Hall,
Newcastle-under-Lyme, Staffs.

My Dear Mr. Mayor,

It was with no little confidence that we assured the mothers and children evacuated from this Borough of the welcome and assistance that would be accorded to them at the end of their journey. Experience has shown adequate justification for that confidence.

I have been deeply moved by the reports which have reached me, both from those who conducted the parties and from the evacuees themselves. They reveal the abundance of thought and consideration given by you and your officers to the arrangements necessary for the reception of the mothers and children, and the kindheartedness with which you have all been actuated.

To have been received and cared for in such a manner has meant more than I can say to those of our folk who have been uprooted, while for those left behind, the relief that their families are now in a safer area is coupled with the knowledge that everything possible is being done for their welfare.

I find it difficult to give suitable expression to our thanks to you and your helpers for all your kindness, but I shall be glad if you will convey our grateful appreciation to all those who have given such willing assistance.

Yours sincerely,

G. J. SCOTT,

Mayor.

Evacuees. A letter from the mayor of Hendon, dated 11th August 1944, thanking the mayor of Newcastle for the kind treatment of evacuees sent to Newcastle from London.

Home Guard.   A snapshot of 'Ern, Tony and George', Newcastle Home Guard, 1941.

Civil Defence. Chesterton ARP wardens.

Wartime Scenes (4).   The open market, 'The Stones', taking place as usual in 1943.

SECTION A.

Statistics and Social Conditions of the Area.

Area.

The area of the Borough is 8,882 acres.

Population, etc.

The Registrar-General's estimate of the population for 1944 is 63,360.

The number of inhabited houses at the end of 1944 was 18,978.

Rateable Value, etc.

The rateable value of the Borough is £308,411, and one penny rate in the £ (General Rate) produces £1,167 exclusive of voids, etc.

War-Time Nurseries.

In the Borough there are six War-Time Day Nurseries and one Residential Nursery organised by the Corporation under the aegis of the Ministry of Health. In these nurseries there is accommodation for 280 children.

Social Conditions—Unemployment.

With regard to the extent of unemployment, I am indebted to the Manager of the Employment Exchange for the following information. The average weekly unemployment figure for the Newcastle-under-Lyme area during 1944 was 340, as compared with 181 for the year 1943. The present figure is approximately 1.7% of the insured population of 20,000 (estimated), as against .9% for 1943, .91% for 1942, 1.3% for 1941, 6.6% for 1940, 19.6% for 1939, 20% for 1938, 17% for 1937, 20% for 1936, 23% for 1935, 22% for 1934, 25% for 1933, and 37% for 1932.

Extracts from Vital Statistics for the Year.

		Total	Male	Female	Rate	
Live Births	Legitimate	1311	679	632	21.88	per 1000 estimated population
	Illegitimate	75	43	32		
Stillbirths		59	28	31	40.83	per 1000 total live and still births
Deaths		656	343	313	10.35	per 1000 estimated population

Deaths and death-rates from puerperal causes :—

	Deaths	Rate per 1000 total live & still births
Puerperal and Post-abortive sepsis	3	2.076
Other maternal causes ...	—	—
Total	3	2.076

Death-rate of Infants under 1 year of age per 1,000 live births :—

Total	40.4
Legitimate	38.14
Illegitimate... ...	80.

Deaths from Cancer (all ages)	101
Deaths from measles (all ages)	2
Deaths from whooping cough (all ages) ...	2
Deaths from diarrhoea (under 2 years of age)	3

Wartime Statistics.   Proving that the war reduced unemployment!

Military Parade (1).   A military band approaching the
town along Liverpool Road. No more details are known.

On Parade. A rare photograph of the Benbow Divisional Guard on parade at the front of Clayton Hall (camouflaged). The officer in charge was Lt. E. Hendy.

Military Parade (2).　　The Home Guard on parade in Newcastle High Street, late 1944.

Wartime Scenes (5).   The Dunkirk of Newcastle! Although no fighting took place on these beaches. The building in the background (in front of St Giles Church) was used by the Fleet Air Arm.

Civil Defence Sports Gala. Taken on 4th September 1943 on the Wolstanton Grammar School playing fields, this photograph shows contestants in the dog show.

Wartime Scenes (6). The junction of London Road and Penkhull Street. The advertisement reads 'Hitler desires the world but you can have it with a Bush radio.' The Boat and Horses, popular with American soldiers, can be seen in the distance (right).

Antipodean Charity. Inside Len Skerrat's off-licence at the top of Chapel Street, Silverdale, the committee for distributing food from Australia examines the victuals destined for the Silverdale old folks (1942).

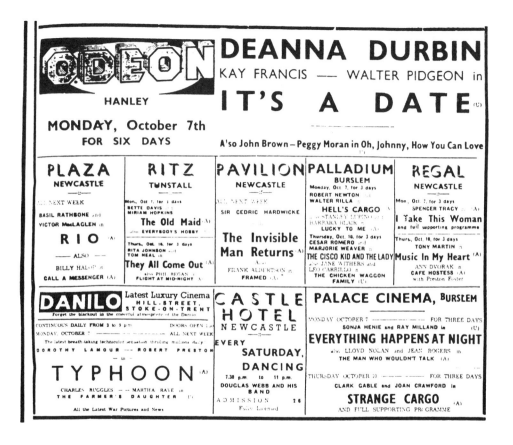

Wartime Entertainment. Advertisement from the *Newcastle Times,* 4th October 1940. Four Newcastle cinemas are featured as well as dancing at the Castle Hotel.

United States Army.   The United States First Army based at Keele Hall under the command of Colonel Stack. Local children used to travel up to Keele where they could retrieve oranges and bananas thrown for them by the U.S. soldiers. The Boat and Horses in Stubbs Gate served as a 'local' for the Americans.

Post-War Planning.   As early as 1943, Borough Council planners were working on their post-war plan for the town. Not a particularly good photograph . . . but very atmospheric.

A Wartime Wedding. The wedding of Mr and Mrs Fox at Silverdale. The photograph was taken by William Parton, a well-known local photographer who was also chairman of the library committee.

Library. The library in the Municipal Hall played a wartime role. In November 1941, twenty volumes on aircraft maintenance and operation were purchased for the use of the Fleet Air Arm and ATCs in the area. There was also a special scheme to provide a reading room for evacuees. (The gentleman in the foreground is William Parton, chairman of the library committee.)

Menu.

□□□□

Cold Beef, Lamb or Pork and Ham.

Salad.

□□□□

Apple Tart and Custard.

OR
□□□□

Cheese and Biscuits.

Cakes.

□□□□

Tea or Coffee.

Cigarettes.

□□□□

Licensed Bar.

Toast List.

□□□□

Proposed by	Responded to by
" The King."	
Chief Warden.	
" The Mayor & Mayoress."	
Divisional Warden (South)	His Worship the Mayor.
J. W. Bentley, Esq.	(Ald. J. H. Ramsbotham, J.P.)
" Emergency Committee & Civic Guests."	
Deputy Chief Warden.	Deputy Mayor
(L. Burchell, Esq.)	(Ald. J. Kelly, J.P.)
" Newcastle-under-Lyme C.D. Wardens' Service."	
Town Clerk & Controller.	The Chief Warden.
(J. Griffith, Esq., M.A., Lt. B.)	(W. E. Williamson, Esq.)
" Police Co-operation."	
Training Officer	The Chief Constable.
R. G. Gater.	(G. S. Jackson, Esq.)
" Lady Visitors."	
Staff Officer	The Mayoress
J. B. Hambleton.	(Mrs. J. H. Ramsbotham)
Toastmaster	G. E. Middleton, Esq.

The End Approaches.   A month or so before the end of the war, Newcastle's Civil Defence wardens had dinner at the Municipal Hall to congratulate themselves on the war effort. The last meeting of the emergency committee took place on 16th October 1945.

Wartime Graffiti. At the end of the war residents of John Street, Newcastle, express their relief.

VE Day. A group of local lads standing by a static tank opposite Garden Street, 1945. From left to right they are: Kathie Corkott, Ray Barlow, Harold Trevor, Sid Smith, Vincent Cornwell, Wilf Barlow, Albert Corkott, Gordon Walters, Pat Gill, Alf Dobson, Stuart Palmer, Jess Johnson.

Hassell Street VE Day Celebrations. A very clear photograph of one of the many street parties held to celebrate victory in Europe, June 1945.

VE Day Celebrations. The Well Street/Garden Street party to celebrate victory. (Can you spot the landlady of one of Newcastle's popular Ironmarket pubs?)

VE Day Celebrations.   Unfortunately, rather a more posed street-party photograph but there's no disguising the happiness of these residents of Heath Street and Enderley Street.

Post-War Surplus. Effra sales at Apedale was opened *c.*1947 by a Mr McCann to deal in Second World War surplus. The company sold refurbished tanks, but was closed early in 1956 after a scandal; armaments were sold to the Israelis via the UK government and to the Egyptians via the Netherlands!